PAMPHLETS ON AMERICAN WRITERS · NUMBER 55

UNIVERSITY OF MINNESOTA

Richard Eberhart

BY RALPH J. MILLS, JR.

UNIVERSITY OF MINNESOTA PRESS · MINNEAPOLIS

Library of Congress Catalog Card Number: 66-63487

Permission to use the excerpts from Richard Eberhart's *Collected Poems
1930–1960* (© 1960) was granted by the publishers, Oxford University Press,
New York, and Chatto & Windus, London. Oxford University Press also granted
permission to use the lines quoted from *The Quarry* (© 1964). The lines from
The Visionary Farms are quoted by permission of the University of North
Carolina Press, publishers of *Collected Verse Plays* (© 1962). Mr. Eberhart
granted permission to quote from *A Bravery of Earth* (copyright 1930).

Distributed to high schools in the United States by Webster Division
McGraw-Hill Book Company
St. Louis   New York   San Francisco   Dallas

PUBLISHED IN GREAT BRITAIN, INDIA, AND PAKISTAN BY THE OXFORD
UNIVERSITY PRESS, LONDON, BOMBAY, AND KARACHI, AND IN CANADA
BY THE COPP CLARK PUBLISHING CO. LIMITED, TORONTO

FOR HELEN AND NATALIE

RALPH J. MILLS, JR., author of *Contemporary American Poetry* and editor of *On the Poet and His Craft: Selected Prose of Theodore Roethke*, is an associate professor of English at the University of Illinois, Chicago Circle.

⤳ *Richard Eberhart*

Anyone surveying the developments in American poetry during the last three decades and noting the emergence of a new and powerfully equipped generation of poets in the period between the middle 1930's and the close of World War II must be attracted immediately by the figure of Richard Eberhart. Born in 1904 at Austin, Minnesota, he is the oldest of three senior poets (the other two are Stanley Kunitz and the late Theodore Roethke) who broke ground for that generation, which also includes Robert Lowell, John Berryman, and Karl Shapiro. But recognition has come to him, as it has to Kunitz and Roethke, slowly and belatedly. Together with them Eberhart explores the possibilities of a personal lyricism enclosing a broad spectrum of human experience and boldly testing the forms and language for articulating what imagination gives and intuition seizes. Dispensing for the most part with the device of the persona or fictional speaker so profitably employed by Eliot, Pound, and Stevens, and lacking any inclination to commit themselves to systematic frameworks of ideas or to build private mythologies to support the imaginative interpretation of experience, these three poets and the others of their generation openly engage the material of their work in fresh, dramatic, and often original ways.

While certain general affinities may be traced among these poets when they are viewed in the perspective of the literary historian, it is not the intention here to look for them. Indeed the individual achievement of a writer such as Eberhart can be seriously distorted if examined through the odd lenses of similarities and relationships, for he has found a prominent place in the generation

5

of which I have been speaking only by traveling an independent route and appearing from a different direction than his contemporaries. In background and youthful experience, in many of the artistic and intellectual influences that contrived to shape his thought and poetry, Eberhart needs to be sharply distinguished from most other American poets of his approximate age. Not easily classifiable, he continues over the years to stand out as a highly individual, sometimes even slightly eccentric poet who is unswervingly dedicated to the life of the imagination and the craft of poetry.

Eberhart studied for a year at the University of Minnesota, then attended Dartmouth, where he received his B.A. in 1926. When he was only eighteen his mother contracted cancer of the lung and suffered a "nine-month birth of death through utmost pain" which he "witnessed intimately" and which became a turning point in his life. Subsequently he wrote that this terrible ordeal was the probable cause of his selection of a poet's career, and in fact his mother's illness and premature death appear several times in poems as well as in one of the verse plays.

Before resuming his studies in England, Eberhart journeyed to the Orient as a steamer hand. In 1929 he was awarded a B.A., in 1933 an M.A. from St. John's College, Cambridge. While at Cambridge he was exposed to the teaching of I. A. Richards and F. R. Leavis; two young poets, Kathleen Raine and William Empson, were students there at the same time. Eberhart read thoroughly the then excitingly new and radical poetry of Gerard Manley Hopkins (whose work did not become available until after World War I), T. S. Eliot, D. H. Lawrence, and other pioneer modernists, but he must have devoted himself equally to the writings of Shakespeare, Donne, Wordsworth, Coleridge, and Shelley. The influence of some of these poets shows, naturally enough, in his earliest verse.

6

From this milieu, rather than an American one, Eberhart launched himself as a poet. His first book, *A Bravery of Earth* (1930), was published in a year which the author spent tutoring the son of King Prajadhipok of Siam — an exotic beginning for a lifetime of service as a teacher of literature and of poetic accomplishment of a high order. From 1933 until 1941 he taught at St. Mark's School, Southboro, Massachusetts, where he met Robert Lowell, then a pupil. During the war Eberhart acted as a naval gunnery officer and instructor, a role which prompted several of his fiercest and most dramatic poems, and afterwards returned to teaching, with a six-year interlude in the business world. Since 1956 he has been a professor of English and Poet in Residence at Dartmouth College, has spent a term as Consultant in Poetry at the Library of Congress; his *Collected Poems 1930–1960* was honored with the Bollingen Prize.

Eberhart's poems set themselves in a curiously singular relationship to established canons of modern poetic practice, which they seldom heed. These poems treat philosophic themes abstractly; their method is frequently deductive rather than inductive, as Philip Booth has persuasively argued; they rely much of the time on inspiration, in the poet's own words, "burst into life spontaneously," during a period in which critical opinion emphasizes careful craftsmanship, the poem as a discovered but also a *made* object; as a final impertinence they are apt to level undisguised moral judgments while still fighting shy of dogma and firmly insisting on the ultimate mysteriousness of existence, the impenetrable heart of reality. In his handling of words Eberhart may be playful and witty, as in this excerpt from a speech in "Triptych," a play for voices:

> Shallow? Then air is shallow,
> Through which we see to heaven.
> Shallow? Then water is shallow,

7

> Of which we are composed.
> Shallow? Then morning's atmosphere,
> Lakes, rivers, rills and streams
> Are shallow. What is your jealous depth
> But layers and layers of shallows?

Or to take one of many possible examples, this from "The Recapitulation," he can be austere and reflective:

> Not through the rational mind,
> But by elation coming to me
> Sometimes, I am sure
> Death is but a door.

Or he can express, with the impatience of anger and disgust, his judgment of the inhumane folly of men in conflict, as in "At the End of War":

> For they cannot think straight, or remember what
>   they said,
> Cannot keep their word,
> Or realize how soon they will be dead,
> Nor distinguish between verities
> Who lust over presences,
> Nor be faithful
> Who are wrathful,
> Nor escape animal passion
> With cross-bow, slit-trench, Napalm bomb, atom
>   bomb.

Or at the opposite end of his emotional range he can become purely lyrical:

> Cover me over, clover;
> Cover me over, grass.
> The mellow day is over
> And there is night to pass.

These passages give a mere sampling of the variety of moods to be found in Eberhart's writing and the language he uses to evoke them. It ought also to be remarked in passing that sometimes emotional pressure or the love of wit exceeds the poet's control and discrimination with consequent faults in diction, tone, and rhythm; but that seems a small price to pay for many successes and for a recognizably original voice. Eberhart's notion of poetic creation, of the act of composition, and of the operations of the poet's mind, all of them so intimately connected with what he conceives to be his essential artistic task, makes him vulnerable to these dangers as well as leading him to an abundance of fine poems. In the following pages we will examine briefly this poetic theory and some of the work which is its concrete manifestation.

To start with, Eberhart thinks of the poem as being, at its highest level, inspirational in origin, an idea which, if not critically popular in our century, has managed to survive as a legacy of the Romantics and has received confirmation in varying degrees by modern poets as different as Rainer Maria Rilke, D. H. Lawrence, Herbert Read, and Robert Graves. Of course it is doubtful that any of these poets would say *each* of his poems arrived in its entirety, bursting upon the mind in a moment of trance-like vision or imaginative possession, nor would Eberhart himself make such a claim; yet all of them could point to some of their best work as originating in luminous instances of this sort. In a response to comments in a recent symposium on one of his own poems Eberhart refers to and quotes Plato's *Ion*. He designates several of his pieces "as coming under this [Platonic] theory of creation": namely " 'Now Is the Air Made of Chiming Balls,' " " 'If I Could Only Live at the Pitch That Is Near Madness,' " "1934," " 'Go to the Shine That's on a Tree,' " and "Only in the Dream." Several others, including "The Groundhog," "Maze," "For a Lamb," and " 'In a Hard Intellectual Light,' " are also cited but are "less purely" the result, in the words of Plato's dialogue, of "falling

9

under the power of music and meter," of being "inspired and possessed." Eberhart does not, however, stop with these disclosures; he goes on to remark how he "grew up in the convictions of ambiguity, ambivalence, and irony as central to poetry and cannot rationally accept Plato's last words 'when [the poet] has not attained to this state, he is powerless and is unable to utter his oracles.' " Thus poems which are *given in their totality* are few and far between, the product of rare occasions of unalloyed inspiration.

Nonetheless the infrequency of poems dictated with no necessity for alteration does not preclude another kind of inspiration at work in the rest of Eberhart's poetry. This second type of inspiration likewise derives from moments of special perceptiveness and extraordinary sensitivity, in short, moments of revelation; but the difference from the first, or higher, inspirational experience lies in the fact that now the dictation is less complete and must be augmented by the poet's conscious efforts. In this case the poem does not come, as it were, gratuitously, and he tries to grasp in an order of language as much as he can of a fleeting intuition before it vanishes. Eberhart's "Notes on Poetry" offers further explanations: "A poet does what he can do. Poetry is dynamic, Protean. In the rigors of composition it seems to me that the poet's mind is a filament, informed with the irrational vitality of energy as it was discovered in our time in quantum mechanics. The quanta may shoot off any way. (You breathe in maybe God.) If you dislike the word inspiration, say then that the poet in a creative state of mind is in a state different from that of his ordinary or logical state. This leads on not to automatic writing, but to some mysterious power latent within him which illuminates his being so that his perceptions are more than ordinarily available for use, and that in such moments he has the ability to establish feelings, ideas and perceptions which are communicable in potential degree and with some pleasure."

Whatever may be felt about the applicability of the analogy with modern physics this passage holds up as one of the best of several statements Eberhart has written insisting upon the poet's unusual condition of attentiveness and receptivity immediately preceding a seizure of creative activity. The validity of his account rests on its experiential nature, for it is quite without theoretical pretensions and simply essays a description at first hand of what happens to Eberhart when he writes a poem. Yet the passage does more than tell us generally how many of his poems come about; we will find on reading through the body of Eberhart's work that the observations here have an additional relevance both to its formal aspects and to its themes. A sense of the processes of his art is indispensable for a full understanding and appreciation of what it attempts.

In view of these procedures in poetic composition, sketched here rather hastily, it should not be surprising to the reader that the primary qualities he notices in Eberhart probably will be spontaneity and the immediate presence of, involvement with, a particular experience. Even *A Bravery of Earth*, which is a book-length autobiographical poem, achieves such effects, though as a whole it is not very satisfactory. Like many initial endeavors with a long poem this one is packed with everything that has seemed important in the writer's life thus far. The book divides into two parts, the first of which, opening with a lovely lyric section, forms a kind of allegory of the self from innocence to experience, from the natural life and the free enjoyment of the senses through the acquaintance with love to the discovery of reason and the shocking knowledge of death. Too often the poet loses himself and control over his material in the currents of his strong but conflicting emotions. Yet the movement of the poem, in spite of its awkwardness and confusion (interspersed with fine, compelling passages), and as Peter Thorslev has said, its obvious indebtedness to Wordsworth, car-

ries the reader along at a rapid pace and impresses on him a sensation of the vital flow of living experience, even if that experience
is not always adequately directed and defined. Of course this sort
of sensation belongs to literature generally, but in Eberhart's case,
as no doubt in others, it makes special claims on our consideration
and endows his poetry with uncommon energy and drama.

Of his long poem Eberhart has retained only three rather brief
portions for inclusion in his *Collected Poems*, and the best of these
is a lyric prologue which I quote in part as evidence of already
estimable gifts:

> This fevers me, this sun on green,
> On grass glowing, this young spring.
> The secret hallowing is come,
> Regenerate sudden incarnation,
> Mystery made visible
> In growth, yet subtly veiled in all,
> Ununderstandable in grass,
> In flowers, and in the human heart,
> This lyric mortal loveliness,
> This earth breathing, and the sun.

In the second half of the poem Eberhart continues his autobiographical narrative but now shifts from the lyrical account of his
affective inner life to a detailed picture of the external world, of
person and place as he meets them on his global voyage, working
aboard a steamer. This transition from inner to outer focus at
last brings about the completion of a pattern in the poet's existence:

> Into the first awareness trembling,
> Girded with mortality;
> Into the second awareness plunging,
> Impaled upon mentality;
> Into the third awareness coming
> To understand in men's action

> Mankind's desire and destiny,
> Youth lies buried and man stands up
> In a bravery of earth.

Looking back on these lines from the poem's conclusion with the advantage of time one is apt to think that while they round off nicely the author's formal intentions here, the three types of awareness he distinguishes are not, as it seems, easily succeeded in later poems by a point of view unhindered by their troubling presence. In fact "mortality," "mentality," and "men's actions" may be said to become Eberhart's chief themes throughout his career. For our purposes we might better read the end of *A Bravery of Earth* as an announcement of things to come, of thematic resources yet to be tapped. With the publication of *Reading the Spirit* (1937) these resources are opened and the long phase of this poet's genuine accomplishment, extending to his newest collection, *The Quarry* (1964), begins. With few exceptions he confines himself after his first book to the short or medium-length poem, kinds more suited to the alternatively meditative and intuitive character of his imagination. Poems of these proportions can more readily approximate to the flashes of perception which usually initiate them. As we know, for Eberhart the poet's primary obligation is to voice the truth disclosed by a specific experience with all the force of the revelation itself, and so it is a note of immediacy or urgency that his poetry most often, if not always, strikes.

Reading the Spirit still contains traces of its author's deep attachment to Wordsworth, coupled with some evidence of Hopkins' influence, in "Four Lakes' Days," and indeed Eberhart has a love for nature, for land- and seascape, that associates him with these two English poets, though he rapidly develops his own manner of treating it. Most apparent in this second book, however, is not a feeling for nature but a terrible intensity of vision, a radical, piercing insight into psychic and spiritual processes reminiscent of Blake, which was hardly to be predicted on the basis of *A Bravery of Earth.* Themes we noted in that poem are now embodied in the dramatic presentation of experiences at once peculiarly individual and clearly universal.

"Maze," for example, starts out as a pastoral poem in which we expect to find a fundamental harmony of man with nature elaborated:

> I have a tree in my arm,
> There are two hounds in my feet,
> The earth can do me no harm
> And the lake of my eyes is sweet.

The unity proclaimed in this stanza is, nonetheless, of short duration; not only has a fire destroyed the tree and a lack of blood starved the hounds but questions of "will" and "a human mind that has bounds" interrupt what was obviously a mode of existence from which intellectual calculation was quite absent. In the third stanza disruption is completed by a more pointed questioning which is answered in oracular fashion in the fourth:

> It is man did it, man,
> Who imagined imagination,
> And he did what man can,
> He uncreated creation.

This leads to a concluding stanza which is an ironic version of the poem's beginning:

> There is no tree in my arm,
> I have no hounds in my feet,
> The earth can soothe me and harm,
> And the lake of my eyes is a cheat.

Undoubtedly the reader will have several ways of interpreting various details in this poem, but puzzling as some things may seem we can be fairly certain of what has been taking place. In archetypal or symbolic terms the poem recounts a fall from innocence, wholeness, and a sort of grace into a state of experience, characterized by the intrusion of self-consciousness, inquisitiveness, and intellectual activity. The maze of the title is what reality becomes after the breakup of the original unity: there the individual, driven by will, relentlessly seeks knowledge.

This theme of "mentality," to use Eberhart's word from *A Bravery of Earth*, appears regularly in his poetry, often in connection with different experiences of knowing. One early poem, "Request for Offering," pursues the theme in a strictly allegorical manner through the figures of a "baleful lion" and "the virgin pap / Of the white world." If seen as showing ferocious intellect poised to attack the beautiful mystery of the cosmos the poem makes sense; it also suggests a violation or rape, so that the intended assault takes on a more specific moral cast. But the poem's direction is halted abruptly in the fourth stanza, where the lion's attack meets a surprising resistance:

> Amaze your eyes now, hard
> Is the marble pap of the world
> And the baleful lion regard
> With the claws of the paw curled.

The next, and final, stanza merely repeats the first one, which utters the "request" for the sacrifice or "offering," the implication being that it will probably be made again and again but that the impenetrability of the world will remain secure.

Another poem, " 'If I Could Only Live at the Pitch That Is Near Madness,' " from Eberhart's third book, *Song and Idea* (1942), examines the same fall from innocence and the unified life into knowledge that we saw in "Maze," but here the emphasis on perception — the childish vision as the clearest and most discerning one — is pronounced. The first two stanzas belong to a tradition in modern poetry, reaching from Blake through Rimbaud to E. E. Cummings and Dylan Thomas, which equates the child's intensity of vision with a hallucinated perception liberated from routine habits of mind that impose a conventional method of looking at the world without ever seeing it:

> If I could only live at the pitch that is near
> madness
> When everything is as it was in my childhood
> Violent, vivid, and of infinite possibility:
> That the sun and the moon broke over my head.
>
> Then I cast time out of the trees and fields,
> Then I stood immaculate in the Ego;
> Then I eyed the world with all delight,
> Reality was the perfection of my sight.

In this instance of enlightenment the visible universe discloses its hidden energies, time is overcome, and selfhood is enjoyed in all of its pristine innocence and completeness. We know from the poem's beginning that this vision does not survive as a constant mode of seeing and experiencing reality; only at extraordinary moments, when the individual approaches the sheer unreason and heightened consciousness of madness, will that kind of perceiving be reawakened. Stanza three makes plain the fact that "the race of mankind" cannot countenance a world where "fields and trees" have "a way of being themselves," and so the child is required to supply "a moral answer" for his vision, to learn the adult's distinction between good and evil, to share the adult's burden of guilt, with disastrous results:

> I gave the moral answer and I died
> And into a realm of complexity came
> Where nothing is possible but necessity
> And the truth wailing there like a red babe.

The poem ends, then, in a confirmation of human misery and torment, in a divided, fateful state very like the confused one with which "Maze" finishes. The "moral answer" brings evil into the child's universe, shattering his unified, positive view. The point should be stressed that the fall from simple harmony with creation and the loss of the vision which is so essential a part of it appears quite unavoidable. As it does for T. S. Eliot, Edwin Muir, Kathleen Raine, and a number of other modern poets, the lapse from grace and wholeness in the child has for Eberhart metaphysical and religious implications prior to any merely psychological effects, though these are not always set forth in specifically Christian terms. Yet the English poet and critic Michael Roberts in his introduction to *Reading the Spirit* remarked that Eberhart's poetry "represents the Western, Christian, Aristotelean view of life against the Oriental and Plotinic view; its music is alert and energetic rather than mellifluous and drowsy; and the delight at which it aims is the delight of intense mental and physical activity, and not of passivity and disembodied ecstasy." This description is quite accurate; only in some of his later poems, of which more presently, does Eberhart contradict it.

Man's fallen condition, his inner disunity, as we have seen it represented in these poems certainly furnishes the poet with a basis for his ambivalent role with regard to his intuitions and for the tension which so often obtains between them. In an autobiographical sketch for *Twentieth Century Authors,* Eberhart calls himself a "dualist" and a "relativist" rather than a "dogmatist." The poet needs to adopt a "sitting on the fence attitude" which "allows him to escape whole decades of intellectual error, while it provides radical use of the deepest subjective states of mind toward vision felt as absolute when experienced." What he trusts is the intuition or perception which comes from the poetic imagination and the sudden unique truth it extends. Such intuitions occasionally conflict with one another, but that is because they emerge from the opposing forces operating in man's divided state. In "Notes on Poetry" Eberhart says: "Divisive man can know unity only at death (or so he can speculate), and he cannot know what kind of unity that is. He lives in continuous struggle with his imperfection and the imperfection of life. If one were only conscious of harmony, there would be no need to write." The relativism of Eberhart therefore consists in a submission to the dictates of each imaginative experience as it takes hold of him without concern for its close agreement with other experiences or with any pre-existing structure of ideas: in Wallace Stevens' words, "The poem is the cry of its occasion." Consequently, while poems might seem to challenge each other in attitude, such apparent inconsistencies should not obscure the poet's larger purpose, which is his endeavor through "vision felt as absolute when experienced" to attain to what deep if partial truths, what glimpses and approximations of a transcendent and, from a limited human position, unfathomable unity, he can.

"The Skier and the Mountain," included in *Undercliff* (1953), is a poem about the difficulties of reaching any firm and final plane of reality, of opening up a clear route of access to the supernatural; it is only one of many poems in which Eberhart proceeds toward the extremes of his "mentality" theme, moving into regions of divinity on the "elusive" and tricky waves of the imagination. Though the visionary events of the poem occur in the midst of a day's skiing, the first line prepares us for them by introducing spiritual realities before physical ones:

> The gods are too airy: feathery as the snow
> When its consistency is just the imagination's,
> I recognize, but also in an airy, gauzy way
> That it will capture me, I will never capture it.
> The imagination is too elusive, too like me.
> The gods are the airiness of my spirit.
> I have dreamed upon them tiptop dreams,
> Yet they elude me, like the next step on the ski.
> I pole along, push upward, I see the summit,

Yet the snow on which I glide is treachery.
The gods are too airy. It is their elusive nature
I in my intellectual pride have wished to know.

We begin with "the gods," and snow, summit, and skis may
strike the reader as obvious metaphorical devices used to support
Eberhart's speculations on the life and activity of the imagination
rather than substantial things in their own right. Up to a point
that interpretation is correct, but only so far as the first stanza is
concerned; the second stanza incarnates the actual experience of
vision, which took place sometime in the past during a skiing expe-
dition. Thus Eberhart has reversed the temporal order in the poem,
perhaps to underline its reflective character: stanza one, composed
in the present tense (with hints of the past: "I have thought I knew
what I was doing"), contains meditations prompted by the experience recounted in stanza two, which is written in the past tense.
To get at the center of the poet's thought here we must also con-
front this experience:

I saw an old country god of the mountain,
Far up, leaning out of the summit mist,
Born beyond time, and wise beyond our wisdom.
He was beside an old, gnarled trunk of a tree
Blasted by the winds. Stones outcropped the snow,
There where the summit was bare, or would be bare.
I thought him a dream-like creature, a god beyond evil,
And thought to speak of the portent of my time,
To broach some ultimate question. No bird
Flew in this flying mist. As I raised my voice
To shape the matters of the intellect
And integrate the spirit, the old, wise god,
Natural to the place, positive and free,
Vanished as he had been supernatural dream.
I was astonished by his absence, deprived
Of the astonishment of his presence, standing
In a reverie of the deepest mist, cloud and snow,

Solitary on the mountain slope: the vision gone,
Even as the vision came. This was then the gods' meaning,
That they leave us in our true humanity,
Elusive, shadowy gods of our detachment,
Who lead us to the summits, and keep their secrets.

The first half of the poem is devoted to affirming the impossibility of coming into close contact with "the gods," who are not only independent beings but are also identified with the ethereal nature of the poet's own spirit. Eberhart recognizes how his "intellectual pride" wishes rationally to conquer and explain these puzzling deities, but the single means of approach is through the imagination, itself an elusive instrument. In fact the "soaring" of the imagination leads to the poet's realization that he is "the captured actor, the taken one" of the gods, and he knows finally that he is "their imagination, lost to self and to will." At the stanza's end pride has melted to "humility."

Stanza two, as we have seen, concentrates on the vision and pursuit of a god. The incident, haunting in the detail Eberhart has given it, provides matter for the more abstract thinking done in the previous stanza and demonstrates the ultimate failure to establish direct relations between man and the divine. Will and reason may be thwarted, but the last lines tell us something important all the same. The gods will not lift us from our "true humanity," Eberhart says there, and this notion serves to enforce his interpretation of the human estate as a fallen, disharmonious one. Yet the gods do compel us "to the summits," stirring our latent fascination for a higher plane of reality while remaining forever mysterious. Whether we assume them to be projections of the poet's imagination or find them to be forms of the supernatural, these gods, by their enigmatic attractions, urge us toward "our detachment," by which I take Eberhart to mean the release and free exercise of the spirit in its quest for enduring truth.

But Eberhart never intends that a quest of this sort shall lose itself in regions where earthly, human nature is alien or forsaken: "the saving grace of a poem may light the reader likewise out of some darkness," he writes in "Notes on Poetry," "and art is essentially social." In " 'The Goal of Intellectual Man' " from *Song and Idea*, one of his poems about the artist's responsibilities, he defines the object of the quest. The "intellectual man," by which term he certainly designates the poet in the broadest sense, seeks "To bring down out of uncreated light/ Illumination to our night," that is, he can aim at a visionary knowledge through the imagination, a knowledge which reflects divinity. The "uncreated light" of the first stanza and the "fire" of the second are both used here and elsewhere as traditionally representative symbols for God or Ultimate Being (see also, for example, the poems "The Incomparable Light" and "A Meditation"). Quite clearly, however, the poet does not wish to possess this divine fire for himself, nor does he desire the annihilation of his own human identity in an absolute. Unlike Prometheus, he does not defy the deity. His "goal" is not, either, a deathly "imageless place,"

> But it is human love, love
> Concrete, specific, in a natural move
> Gathering goodness, it is free
> In the blood as in the mind's harmony,
>
> It is love discoverable here
> Difficult, dangerous, pure, clear,
> The truth of the positive hour
> Composing all of human power.

Love, as Eberhart employs the word here, includes compassion, understanding, a respect for the inviolability of the individual person, an awareness of the abundant beauty of the natural world and all its creatures, the relationship between man and woman, but this true center of feeling and value must encounter inevitably in his work as in his life the strongest opposition. The chief forces of that opposition manifest themselves in those poems which fall under the two other thematic headings mentioned earlier: "mortality" and "men's actions."

Death readily captures prominence as the most obvious opponent to Eberhart's values, and, not surprisingly, we shall see that it blends into the theme of human behavior. Mortality constantly occupies the poet's mind from *A Bravery of Earth* on. Some of this concern stems from the profoundly disturbing experience of his mother's untimely death and her long, agonizing battle against it. While the signs of that terrible initiation never disappear entirely from the poetry, the shocking confrontation with death puts Eberhart in the way of a variety of imaginative considerations of mortality, of the sundering of spirit from body, the separation of the dead from the living. Occasionally he uses a dead animal as an object to draw his mind into meditation on the fate of all creatures. In "For a Lamb" the analogies with man are not stated, but they hardly need suggesting. At the beginning the poet comes upon the carcass of "a putrid lamb,/ Propped with daisies"; the juxtaposition of the mutilated physical body and the indifferent serenity of nature fixes the paradoxical mood of the poem. With the start of the second stanza Eberhart asks a pointed question, the answers to which, if we can call them that, are provokingly ambiguous and end the piece:

> Where's the lamb? whose tender plaint
> Said all for the mute breezes.
> Say he's in the wind somewhere,
> Say, there's a lamb in the daisies.

The question is really that perennial one we ask when faced with the still, emptied body we once knew so full of life: where has that life, that vital being, gone? Eberhart gives us no certain or comforting reply. First he is boldly crude and spiritual at the same time, for in locating the lamb in the wind he is referring both to the offensive stench of the disemboweled carcass which hovers in the air and to the traditional identification of the life principle or spirit with the element of air or the wind. Yet in the final line he withdraws from these subtleties to the only sure answer: the lamb is *there*, he is *that* dead heap lying in the grass and flowers; beyond such facts we cannot go. We should not, however, accept this poem as proof of a settled conviction on the poet's part; we have to remember his avowed artistic method of expressing a subjective intuition as it occurs. Poems "become what one was at the moment of composition."

"The Groundhog," included in the same volume, *Reading the Spirit*, with the elegiac "For a Lamb," also focuses on a dead carcass, but here there is an intense visualization, an elaboration of physical detail and of the poet's response to it, that are missing from the other, much briefer poem. These qualities put it in a line of descent from Baudelaire's terrifying poem "Une Charogne." In the present piece Eberhart finds the groundhog's body lying "amid the golden fields" of June; his accidental discovery resembles that of "For a Lamb." From then on, however, the poem gathers its own very potent dramatic strengths. Drama springs from the tension generated between observing poet and observed object over a considerable period of time, a period marking the gradual disintegration and, at last, the total disappearance of the groundhog's carcass. Watching this process of decay with an extraordinary but very human fascination, the poet leaves us only faintly aware of the transitions in time from one visit to the field to the next; we seem almost to be witnessing the entire decomposition, so intently is the imagination brought to bear upon the actual details of change and their implications. Though the facts of violent death are presented bluntly in "For a Lamb," they are set forth in an objective, ironical manner which is in distinct contrast to

23

the mode of presentation in "The Groundhog." The poet's reaction to the corpse now is instantaneous; he appears startled not merely by what he has unexpectedly found but also by a piercing realization of its significance for himself as a creature: "Dead lay he; my senses shook,/ And mind outshot our naked frailty."

Aroused by what he sees, the poet obsessively decides to investigate further the relentless progress of destruction:

> There lowly in the vigorous summer
> His form began its senseless change,
> And made my senses waver dim
> Seeing nature ferocious in him.
> Inspecting close his maggots' might
> And seething cauldron of his being,
> Half with loathing, half with a strange love,
> I poked him with an angry stick.
> The fever arose, became a flame
> And Vigour circumscribed the skies,
> Immense energy in the sun,
> And through my frame a sunless trembling.
> My stick had done nor good nor harm.

The aggressive gesture with the stick stirs the maggots to a fury of activity; but the poet is suddenly exposed to an awakening still more frightening, for the seething energy about the corpse releases in him an almost hallucinatory sensation of nature's all-consuming power which brings in its wake a fearful comprehension of the precariousness of his own personal existence. In spite of his terror Eberhart's fascination is hypnotic and complete; he stays rooted to the spot, "watching the object, as before." At length the efforts to calm himself, to master the curious "passion of the blood" aroused in him by the awful vision of decomposition, fail, and he kneels, "praying for joy in the sight of decay." The dark and fiery god of nature, the pantheistic "Vigour," has won his submission.

In the space of the next two lines several months pass; the season turns to autumn and the poet "strict of eye" revisits the groundhog, "the sap gone out" of it and only "the bony sodden hulk" remaining. His attitude has likewise altered, his passionate response become a slightly aloof thoughtfulness:

> But the year had lost its meaning,
> And in intellectual chains
> I lost both love and loathing,
> Mured up in the wall of wisdom.

Eberhart implies in this passage that the first jolting vision of disintegration has robbed the year and its seasons of their sense — that is, the rhythm and pattern of time in his perception of them dissolve into chaos — and has deprived him of his feelings: his whole being is now subordinate to the shattering knowledge of death and reabsorption by nature's thriving energies. "Wisdom," as Eberhart applies the word in this poem, consists in knowing death and guilt; it signifies the knowledge discussed earlier as integral to the descent from innocence to experience. On this occasion the same kind of knowledge is equally crippling because it traps the poet in his intellect, a life-denying bondage.

Two more returns to the scene of the groundhog's death, one in the following summer, the other three years later, occur before the poem's climactic finish. The first of these summer days, "massive and burning, full of life," recalls the previous June, the time of the poet's discovery, but the atmosphere of the day contrasts noticeably with the barren appearance of the animal's remains when Eberhart has again "chanced upon the spot" (the word "chanced" suggests that while his original encounter with the dead groundhog imposed upon him a heavy burden of knowledge not readily disposed of, he may still have forgotten the object which was its cause until he found it once more during a walk):

> There was only a little hair left,
> And bones bleaching in the sunlight
> Beautiful as architecture;
> I watched them like a geometer,
> And cut a walking stick from a birch.

The bones retain hardly a semblance of the flesh and blood they once structured; Eberhart scrutinizes them dispassionately as he would something formally pleasing but nevertheless coldly abstract. Around him nature hums and blazes with renewed vitality and with an abundance whose price is death and anonymity.

Perhaps it is this dreadful combination, the loss of life and the loss of any indication that a particular life was ever lived, which hastens Eberhart to a resurgence of emotion at the end. After three years "there is no sign of the groundhog," though the poet stays standing in the midst of a "whirling summer," nature's eternal return. He cannot avoid feeling the life drying up in him as it has done in that animal carcass; the terrible human message of his experience breaks in waves upon his consciousness: how long is memory, how can civilization or individual achievement finally endure?

> I stood there in the whirling summer,
> My hand capped a withered heart,
> And thought of China and of Greece,
> Of Alexander in his tent;
> Of Montaigne in his tower,
> Of Saint Theresa in her wild lament.

To the emotional outburst of these last lines Eberhart has no counterbalance of reasoned explanation, nor can he satisfy himself as Yeats does in "Lapis Lazuli" and elsewhere with a pose of desperate Nietzschean gaiety at the spectacle of civilizations collapsing and being replaced: such theoretical apparatus is alien to his poetry. Death holds a central, unquestioned position in his imagination, and its relationship to the endless cycle of nature remains visible throughout his work. Even in a very recent poem, "Sea Burial from the Cruiser *Reve*" included in *The Quarry*, dispersal into and assimilation by the elements seems quite appropriate for something which originated with them. In this case Eberhart is actually writing about the ceremony of scattering the ashes of a boat he had owned, but he never tells us so (Denis Donoghue's interview with the poet and Philip Booth's essay on him both contain helpful material for reading the poem). Plainly the ritual and the transformation from one pair of elements to another which it denotes would also be applicable to human ashes, and in spite of knowledge to the contrary we shall, I believe, continue to read the poem as if its subject were indeed a human burial:

> She is now water and air,
> Who was earth and fire.
>
> *Reve* we throttled down
> Between Blake's Point and Western Isle,
>
> Then, oh, then, at the last hour,
> The first hour of her new inheritance,
>
> We strewed her ashes over the waters,
> We gave her the bright sinking
>
> Of unimaginable aftermaths,
> We followed her dispersed spirit
>
> As children with a careless flick of wrist
> Cast on the surface of the sea
>
> New-cut flowers. Deeper down,
> In the heavy blue of the water,
>
> Slowly the white mass of her reduced bones
> Waved, as a flag, from the enclosing depths.
>
> She is now water and air,
> Who was earth and fire.

Eberhart's artistic interest in this relationship of death and nature does not always show itself with the dramatic power of "The Groundhog" but can be lyrical and elegiac, as the lines above prove. So far each of the poems we have looked at keeps the treatment of death to the material and historical levels and refuses to venture beyond them. On such a basis death appears absolute, but that is merely a partial view, easily contradicted by our previous examination of poems directed toward experience of a visionary or mystical order.

Death never really loses its essential strangeness of appeal for Eberhart, and in a number of poems he does attempt imaginatively to trespass its shadowy, indefinite boundaries. In "Grave Piece" and " 'Imagining How It Would Be to Be Dead' " he tries, as Dylan Thomas does in certain of his early poems, to envisage his own dissolution. The concluding lines of both pieces leave the poet poised on the threshold of a spiritual reality, but before he arrives at that stage it is necessary for him to participate through a moment of vivid imaginative possession in the process of decay imposed by death. The earliest of the two poems, "Grave Piece," from *Song and Idea*, is somewhat encumbered by the influence of Hopkins, Blake, and Empson, though the authenticity of perception cannot be denied:

> There in the vasy tomb of bone-green icicles,
> And gelid grasses of cold bruise to touch;
> Of looking roots, night agate eyed . . .

This excruciating process ends with a liberating and transcendent vision in which the poet sees growing "A crystal Tear/ Whose centre is spiritual love." The second poem, collected in *Burr Oaks* (1947), has that unabashed directness of speech that is so compelling a feature of Eberhart's work. In this poem the imagined death consists of an expansion and transformation of self dominated by one element, air, and from the outset it is presented as a desirable rather than a difficult or terrifying series of events. The weight of time, consciousness of which comes as a consequence of the fall from innocence and the disappearance of the child's vision, is thrown off as the body itself disperses into the air and the omnipresent nature of that element is enjoyed:

> I lost my head, and could not hold
> Either my hands together or my heart
> But was so sentient a being
> I seemed to break time apart
> And thus became all things air can touch
> Or could touch could it touch all things,
> And this was an embrace most dear,
> Final, complete, a flying without wings.

The concluding lines clarify the release into a further dimension of spiritual reality, but the poem halts at the frontiers, so to speak, of what is felt yet stays unseen and intangible. Eberhart must rest content to point the direction in which his experience has taken him, for language too has its limits and is attached to the world of things:

> From being bound to one poor skull,
> And that surrounded by one earth,
> And the earth in one universe forced,
> And that chained to some larger gear,
> I was the air, I was the air,
> And then I pressed on eye and cheek
> The sightless hinges of eternity
> That make the whole world creak.

The poem "A Meditation," published in *Song and Idea*, does, however, project itself daringly beyond the borders of mortal existence; in form it is the monologue of a dead man who addresses a living person through his skull, probably discovered by the latter in some ancient ruin or graveyard, though such details are irrelevant to the piece. While it is not stated, we understand that the individual who holds the skull wishes it could yield up its secrets to him. But true to what we have already remarked about Eberhart's attitudes the emphasis of the monologue falls on life, on what should be found there before it vanishes, rather than on any secrets which the dead can disclose:

> I cannot get back, cannot reach or yearn back,
> Nor summon love enough, nor the intellectual care —
> Being dead, you talk as if I had spirit at all —
> To come back to you and tell you who I am.

He places the responsibility for prophesying on his listener, who is still among the living, who is yet "full of imagination" and can create images beyond himself: oracular and speculative activities "can only be talked of by men," for those ideas belong exclusively to earthly existence. The speaker lightly chides the living man for his intellectual labors and their remoteness from the truth, then offers him a *momento mori* in the repeated line: "Life blows like the wind away."

As the poem proceeds and the speaker stresses the perennial "wish" of man "to know/ What it is all about, meaning and moral dimension," we are brought nearer to a glimpse of supernatural reality. This revelation is comprised mostly of warnings about the utter difference between the human estate and the pure life of the spirit existing in a region completely foreign to earthly experience. A total transformation apparently separates the two realms of being, and the mortal flesh shrinks from this frightening change, as the voice of the dead speaker declares:

> You would withdraw in horror at my secret,
> You would not want to know, your long-lashed eyes
>   aglare,
> Of the cold absolute blankness and fate of death,
> Of the depths of being beyond all words to say,
> Of your profound or of the world's destiny,
> Of the mind of God, rising like a mighty fire

> Pure and calm beyond all mortal instances
> Magnificent, eternal, Everlasting, sweet and mild.

In this passage, with its visionary perception, we find once again the confirmation of Eberhart's fundamental religiousness. His convictions are often tested and shaken by tragic or brutal circumstances, by agonies of doubt and questioning; nevertheless they hold firm against these storms of experience, touchstones of belief to which the poet continues to return. The lasting riddle of death and of man's situation afterwards is no further unveiled than we have seen; the stanza below enunciates the obligation to live out the human span in human terms. The difficult but "simple truth" is

> That you are to be man, that is, to be human,
> You are imperfect, will never know perfection,
> You must strive, but the goal will recede forever,
> That you must do what the great poets and sages say,
> Obeying scripture even in the rotten times . . .

Of course death will close out each life and let it "blow like the wind away." In the final stanza the speaker explains the value of his listener's "solemn meditation" on mortality as an enterprise that should lead him back to "seek among [his] fellow creatures whatever is good in life." As before, Eberhart directs the results of spiritual vision to the conditions of existence in *this* world.

The utilization of visionary or mystical experience to illuminate life here and now, and, more particularly, the emphatic sounding of moral imperatives in the concluding portions of "A Meditation" bring that poem near in spirit to the third category of Eberhart's work: "men's actions." I have indicated how he frequently and unashamedly adopts the role of moralist and critic, a role usually disowned in theory by modern poets but one very evident in their practice. Eberhart's best known works as a moralist are, rightfully, his war poems, surely among the finest and most outspoken pieces of that variety in American literature, but his achievement in other areas should not be neglected: his judgments of contemporary society also merit our consideration.

If some authors of excellent poems about World War II — Randall Jarrell and John Ciardi are exemplary in this respect — write from actual combat experience and from the point of view of the soldier or airman totally immersed in war or in the military life, Eberhart chooses the transcendent, objective role of the prophet or seer-poet who envisages the conflict in terms of moral absolutes and of all humanity. War looked at from this position is a cosmic event drawing into play the larger forces of good and evil in the universe and exhibiting to men—should they notice it—their basic imperfection, their underlying savage desire for complete destruction. The adoption of a vatic mask might seem to the skeptical reader an easy way to handle the problematic matter of warfare in poetry, but I think this interpretation would be wrong. No voice is more difficult to raise and to sustain authentically in a poem than the prophetic one, which requires great skill and imagination for its realization. Thus Eberhart's technique must function smoothly and effortlessly, as it were, within the period of inspirational seizure that is germane to his method of poetic production; if it does not the poem may develop rough or awkward spots, however pure the inspiration. Similarly an excess of emotion, of outrage at man's evil, or of abstract thinking can severely damage a poem of this sort — and does so in several instances.

We may take here the justly famous and moving poem "The Fury of Aerial Bombardment" in *Burr Oaks* to exhibit Eberhart's prophetic manner at its best. The poet starts off the first stanza exaltedly, on a cosmic plane boldly challenging God for His apparent refusal to intervene in the affairs of men and to put an end to the viciousness and slaughter of war:

> You would think the fury of aerial bombardment
> Would rouse God to relent; the infinite spaces

Are still silent. He looks on shock-pried faces.
History, even, does not know what is meant.

You would feel that after so many centuries
God would give man to repent; yet he can kill
As Cain could, but with multitudinous will,
No farther advanced than in his ancient furies.

The use of the "you" in these two stanzas is a brilliant stroke because it establishes contact between poet and reader at the same
time that it serves as part of an opening passage of vigorous rhetori-
cal appeal.

Having called upon "history" in general and the figure of Cain,
the first murderer, to support the portrayal of man's age-old desire
to kill rather than love his brother (the implied contrast between
the single murder committed by Cain and the wholesale killing
accomplished by the latest inventions of war is, of course, inten-
tionally disturbing), Eberhart begins to wonder if God is after
all simply "indifferent"; this third stanza closes with the somber
thought that "the eternal truth" perhaps consists only of "man's
fighting soul/ Wherein the Beast ravens in its own avidity." Such
a question really means to ask if God exists at all: should the answer be negative, the inner malice of mankind emerges as the ultimate, eternal reality. But if the poet poses this question he does
not pretend to give a reply of any general sort; instead the last
stanza of the poem moves suddenly into the realm of the particular, borrowing from Eberhart's personal acquaintance:

Of Van Wettering I speak, and Averill,
Names on a list, whose faces I do not recall
But they are gone to early death, who late in school
Distinguished the belt feed lever from the belt
    holding pawl.

Even the relatively specific character of these lines is not per-
mitted to do more than modify a bit the aloofness and exaltation

of the poet's speech, and then only to drive home his point in another way. The oddly formal construction of this one-sentence stanza strengthens the feeling of distance maintained in spite of the introduction of personal details and names. Various meanings may be attributed to the stanza: possibly most important is the shock which occurs in shifting from the universal, philosophical level of the three preceding stanzas to the frank, objective enumeration of facts — the deaths of certain named individuals. The ravening "Beast" abruptly takes on real and deadly proportions: its victims are listed.

The religious or metaphysical implications of the poem are not, as I have said, brought to any conclusive formulation, nor should we expect them to be when we remember Eberhart's avowed dedication to the truth of each poetic vision as he receives it. With that commitment in mind we should also observe that other poems than the present one ("New Hampshire, February" and "Reality! Reality! What Is It?" are two of them) assert with great forthrightness the moments of deepest doubt, of religious belief assaulted by seemingly chance fatefulness. Over against the poems of metaphysical anguish, which originate in the crushing pressure of events on the poet's reason and conscience, one has to set the larger bulk of poetry that surpasses suffering, injustice, and doubt to approach the zone of what Eberhart calls "Psyche." In one of several lectures he has delivered on Will and Psyche in poetry he defines the latter: "Psyche poetry pertains to the soul, to peace, quiet, tranquillity, serenity, harmony, stillness and silence. It provides psychic states of passive pleasure." We will recall how Michael Roberts indicated that the young Eberhart avoided this style, but in recent years he has produced with some frequency poems representative to one degree or another of the category. These poems coincide with their author's intellectual and artistic maturity, with an attitude of calm reflectiveness, and with the contemplation through a number of suggestive terms and images ("light," "love," "unity," "the unfound beyond," "height," or, taken altogether, "God") of a transcendent reality, a divine source.

By way of contrast, Eberhart's war poems belong to the class of "Will poetry," as do his other pieces which express a moral view of human behavior. "Will poetry exists because of the power in the cell beyond its energy to maintain itself. Will results in action, through wish, zeal, volition, passion, determination, choice, and command. Will makes something happen in poetry." Not all Will poems, occupied with men's actions, employ the vatic manner of "The Fury of Aerial Bombardment." Eberhart takes the part both of intimate witness and of commentator in "Fragment of New York, 1929" from *Undercliff*, which has as its chief metaphor for the cold, vicious character of modern society the slaughtering and butchering of animals. The poet begins with an early morning awakening and depicts himself as the city-dweller, whose movements are habitual and mechanical, whose awareness of his own identity is often shaky, who fears the direction in which his thought will lead him. As he goes out into the pre-dawn urban streets under "the one untormented integer," the "surprise moon, four-thirty moon," he feels as if he were going "into Hell again."

In subsequent stanzas Eberhart's graphic rendering of the routines of the slaughterhouse creates a highly charged symbolic vision of contemporary life, of those buried desires and antagonisms that seek their fulfillment in the act of killing. We can elicit for ourselves a variety of topical analogies with the actualities of twentieth-century history — with concentration camps, city gangs, or the sick fantasies of the mass media. The poet gives us a shockingly effective image of our sex and death obsessions in the figure of the beasts' executioner at his daily task:

> The killer's face! He is baffled now,
> Seems. Moment. He poises

> The tip of the knife at the throat.
> So little is life. He cannot make
> The one swift entry and up-jab.
> Curious copulation, death-impregnation.

As if indeed this nightmare experience were a journey into hell, Eberhart ends his poem with indications of emergence and rebirth:

> Death I saw,
> And wormed through it. And make fragment
> Of the end of a time, when seethed
> So thick the life, it knew not,
> In savage complexity, modernity,
> The harsh omnipotence of evil.

Obvious reference is made here to the time specified in the poem's title: the year of the stock market crash, the beginning of the Depression, the finish of a frenzied postwar era. But the substance of the poem has no more special relevance to that period than it does to the present day; rather it fashions a general picture of inhumanity and spiritual vacuity.

If we want to see Eberhart's definite handling of the quality of life in American society at a certain level, then we must turn to the play *The Visionary Farms*, which is, in addition, his most ambitious and successful effort as a verse dramatist. Denis Donoghue, who has discussed the play shrewdly and at length, speaks of it as "expressionist" in style, "a *drame à thèse* . . . with a difference"; the difference lies in the fact that while Eberhart pictures the triumph and failure of a huge business empire and the three men who are its executives he does not attack his material in the spirit of naturalism or social realism but blends elements of fantasy and extravagant comedy with, as he has said himself, "a study of evil Will in a man" and the insidious temptations of money and success, the American dream ("Money is stronger than life, Adam, much stronger," the president of the company tells his vice-president, a man whom he is about to ruin and whose wife is dying). The conventions of realism are further avoided by the poet's use — common to almost all of his plays — of a group of characters, including the Consulting Author, who gather on the stage as in a living room to joke, talk, pun, and finally to watch the play *The Visionary Farms*; but the Consulting Author puts the group under a spell so that they become more than an audience: they are metamorphosed into the actors of the drama they came to see:

> Each thus becomes a part of Everyman.
> What is, is what might happen to him.
> And each can share in the scenes of fabulous life
> As if imagination were reality,
> For reality is strange as imagination.

Considered from another angle, the portion of "reality" in the play is not negligible, for the plot is clearly grounded in the experience of Eberhart's father, a businessman who, his son wrote, "was betrayed by the notorious Cy Thompson, who embezzled over a million dollars" from George A. Hormel and Company, of which Eberhart senior was vice-president. Here he has been developed into the character of Adam Fahnstock, secretary and vice-president of the Parker Corporation, a soap manufacturer. During the course of the play his wife, Vine, is discovered to have an incurable cancer. The main figure is not Fahnstock, though, but "Hurricane" Ransome, the company treasurer, a man of extraordinary business daring whose wild ideas and enormous expenditures (marvelously and wittily caricatured by Eberhart), have brought the firm very high sales and have made him, Fahnstock, and the president, Roger Parker, rich men.

Yet things are not all they seem. The play opens with Ransome giving a Sunday School sermon to the children of the small midwestern town in which the company's employees and executives live. He shows them a silver dollar — "See how clean it is, hard and pure" — as "a symbol of the American dream," and then by thrusting the coin into hydrochloric acid, where it turns "black, fuming," demonstrates how "If you do evil, your soul will turn black/ Immediately, like this hideous dollar." A silver dollar makes an odd symbol for the soul and prepares us for what follows. As the play continues we learn that Ransome is, ironically enough, very like that blackened dollar himself. Though a man prodigiously gifted, he has become inwardly warped; over a number of years he has embezzled increasingly large sums of money from the company and by clever maneuvering of the accounts has kept his thievery hidden. "Success," Ransome remarks at one point, "is a trick," and the trickery exacts a destructive price of the spirit and of human dignity. What started as a relatively harmless borrowing of five dollars from the company has expanded into a monumental swindle. The Visionary Farms, an extraordinary venture in chicken-farming, is invented by Ransome simply as another means of keeping money circulating, the books balanced, and his robbery concealed; thus the American dream of fantastic financial success appears to be a crippling delusion. As Ransome confesses to himself, echoing *King Lear* by the way:

> It is the evil getting me from the inside.
> The slightest, innocent-seeming insinuation
> When it all began, back in 1914,
> Has grown in my hand to my most monstrous sin.
> I am bound upon a wheel of fire.
> There is no end to the agony I am in.

Ransome's crime is uncovered by the president's son, and the calculating executive is imprisoned; with hilarious irony Eberhart has him at the play's finish ruling the prison and its warden with the same energetic business daring and hocus-pocus as he lavished on the Parker Company and his surrealist chicken farms. Ransome typifies an indefatigable American desire for success, fortune, manipulative powers; and while Eberhart shows us this embezzler reaching a tragic moment of self-recognition we still find that his knowledge does not in any fashion curb his basic impulses or cause him to change.

Differing noticeably from Ransome, the figure of Adam Fahnstock stands out as representative of innocence, good will, endurance, victimization, love, and loss. Not only is his wife dying but he is forced at last to relinquish his stock in the company to Parker, a move by which the latter betrays Fahnstock's friendship and ruins him financially. Success for Mr. Parker, or the next thing to it, the salvaging of his honor, is also a trick. Fahnstock remains the embodiment of genuine values in the play; in a scene in his apple orchard he is compelled to explain to his children the impending death of their mother and the collapse of his fortunes. Against the fateful circumstances that have overtaken them and the death which will intrude upon one of them prematurely Adam proposes the single worthy countermeasure:

> While there is love there can be no death
> For we carry love with us to our own end.
> Love we carry in our memories.

In an earlier poem, "Orchard," from *Song and Idea* Eberhart composed a somewhat different version of the disclosure of his mother's mortal illness. There the mother is herself present; she and her husband are cognizant of what must come, but the children can merely guess it from the extremely troubled atmosphere surrounding them. The two brothers are "placed in the first light/ Of brutal recognition," though their sister registers the disturbance without comprehending its source. The concluding stanza elevates the forces in conflict within this family group to a stage at which they exemplify, as they do in *The Visionary Farms*, the inescapable vicissitudes of life and the human will to meet

them. These lines from the poem help us to perceive the role of
Fahnstock and his family, as well as his sturdy opposition to cheat-
ing, greed, and misfortune, in the play:

> And in the evening, among the warm fruit trees
> All of life and all of death were there,
> Of pain unto death, of struggle to endure,
> And the strong right of human love was there.

Eberhart's experiments in the theater, all of them rather recent
(with the exception of the brief "Triptych" they date from 1950
when he began to work in earnest on verse drama), have had some
interesting effects on his poetry too. These are most evident in
his latest collection, *The Quarry*, where, besides poems of philosophical speculation, elegies, and visionary lyrics, one finds an
assortment of pieces unusual in Eberhart's writing: letters in
verse (to W. H. Auden and the late William Carlos Williams),
dramatic monologues utilizing fictional speakers ("A New England Bachelor," "A Maine Roustabout," "The Lament of a New
England Mother") or character sketches ("Ruby Daggett"), and
dialogues which are indeed miniature dramas ("Father and Son,"
"Father and Daughter"). The high quality of these poems indi-
cates yet another direction in which Eberhart's free and generous
imagination may operate.

In spite of such influences deriving from his experiments with
verse drama, however, the predominant trait of Eberhart's later
poetry is of another kind. I am referring to the reflective or Psyche
poems, in which the author contemplates sympathetically and
dispassionately the nature of life, the function of his art, the full
spectrum of experience discussed here under separate and partial
thematic headings of perception, death, and human behavior.
Not all of this poetry fits into the category of Psyche of course, but
much of it does, to use Eberhart's own words, because it "works
partially through a religious attitude." Progression away from the

world of desire and act toward the lasting realities of spirit, toward contemplation entered upon for its own sake or for the sake of vision alone, without any wish to turn the experience to practical account, is characteristic of the purer types of Psyche poem. "Life as a Visionary Spirit," a recent piece from his *Collected Poems*, exhibits this mood of the imagination but also contains certain inherent qualifications of the mood, for Eberhart never produces the absolutely pure Psyche poem:

> Nothing like the freedom of vision,
>   To look from a hill to the sea,
> Meditating one's bile and bible: free
>   From action, to be.
>
> The best moment is when
>   Stillness holds the air motionless,
> So that time can bless
>   History, blood is a caress.
>
> Neither in landwork nor in seawork
>   Believe. Belief must be pure.
> Let the soul softly idle,
>   Beyond past, beyond future.
>
> Let it be said, "A great effulgence
>   Grows upon the sandspit rose.
> A rare salt harrows the air.
>   Your eyes show divine shows."

Though retaining some traces of place, of the physical cosmos, at the start, this poem departs in the third stanza for the world of spirit or psyche, for the regions outside time, for a reality beyond what is immediate to the senses, and advocates a passivity of the soul as the way of attaining such a superior state of being. The realm of appearances, though substantial in itself, becomes illusory if it is believed in as *all* that exists, yet Eberhart neither ignores nor tries to do away with it. The human and the particular, if we look, are stubbornly there, merging and exchanging themselves with the spiritual: while touched with unearthly radiance, the rose in the final stanza keeps its natural identity; the air, element of the spirit, is cut by the salt of the sea; and the manifestations of the divine are seen mirrored in a pair of human eyes. These persistent attachments to earth, even in Psyche poems, put us in mind once again of Eberhart's feeling for location, for man's position in the middle kingdom of the natural world. He writes very accurately of his attitude in the last two stanzas of "Autumnal":

> We have been living the full year,
> It is still full, it is here
> In the late recline of sun,
> A grand red one.
>
> What is going on beyond
> I have not found, am bound
> To the love of the unfound
> Beyond, but here.

The first of these stanzas purposefully recalls the poetry of Wallace Stevens, not only in diction and tone but in attitude; the view expressed closely resembles Stevens' statements about the earthly paradise, about life lived to its completion within the precincts of the material universe and transfigured by the powers of the imagination. I think there can be no doubt that Eberhart also wishes to evoke feelings of fulfillment with regard to life in this world: earlier stanzas of the poem dwell on nature's richness, on the details of creation, praising both their multiplicity and their beauty. These feelings he communicates are ones which he obviously shares with Stevens. But the closing stanza of "Autumnal" marks an unequivocal return by Eberhart to his own voice and to the balance between earthly and visionary commitment which, as frequently noted in this essay, he never fails to hold. Eberhart, with the onset of his later years ("the late recline of the sun"), joins Stevens in approving the profusion of gifts extended by creation even as he travels toward death; however, where Stevens limits reality to the physical world and the work of imagination within it, Eberhart reaffirms his acquaintance with a transcendent and divine reality which he may be incapable of penetrating altogether but which is not less real to him for that.

Eberhart continues in a number of these more recent poems to test, by thought and meditation or in the sudden disclosure by an observed scene or event of a previously unrecognized significance, the extent and validity of that acquaintance. Some of the best pieces are, like "Life as a Visionary Spirit" and "Autumnal," representatives of the Psyche poem, though again they are perhaps less than pure examples of their type because they too hold firmly to images of the natural world. In "Light from Above" Eberhart stands alone on an October afternoon in the "vigor and majesty of the air," which is "empurpled" by rays of sunlight showing through wind-blown clouds onto the landscape he surveys. This light, first described as "the imperial power / Greater than man's works," becomes as the poem proceeds the visible manifestation of a transcendental "unity" for the poet, who has already confessed himself to be delighted by "unsymbolic gestures of eternity." (I gather "unsymbolic" means here something natural as opposed to something designed or imagined by man.) At its conclusion this poem — and we could profitably read it along with "The Illusion of Eternity," from *Selected Poems 1930–1965*, which has similarities of season, setting in nature, and timelessness — rises toward an affirmation in which the natural and supernatural blend before the poet's eye in the actual scene witnessed:

> here, the great sky,

> Full of profound adventure beyond man's losses,
> Tosses the locks of a strong, abrasive radiance

> From the beginning, and through the time of man,
> And into the future beyond our love and wit,
>
> And in the vigor and majesty of the air
> I, empurpled, think on unity
>
> Glimpsed in pure visual belief
> When the sky expresses beyond our powers
>
> The fiat of a great assurance.

Given his methods of composition and his understanding of what, in his own practice, the poem is, we can hardly expect him to claim for his work the coherent structure of a total aesthetic universe, and of course he does not do so. Yet much in his work compensates for its absence. Reading and rereading his poems one comes to recognize — and to appreciate more completely each time — the marvelous and fruitful vantage point he has secured for himself as an artist; this vantage point is actually a condition of the lyric poet's inner life or consciousness and its primary quality remains throughout his career an independent availability to experience which permits him to embrace with equal ardor and sympathy the events of existence in the world and the revelations of the spirit. This position, with all its risks and uncertainties, cannot have been an easy one to maintain over the years, but Eberhart has been amply rewarded in the poetry that has resulted from it. The end of "The Incomparable Light," the poem with which he concludes his *Collected Poems 1930–1960*, should keep us reminded of Eberhart's constant dedication:

> The light beyond compare is my meaning,
> It is the secret source of my beginning,
> Issuance of uniqueness, signal upon suffering,
> It is the wordless bond of all endings,
> It is the subtle flash that tells our song,
> Inescapable brotherhood of the living,
> Our mystery of time, the only hopeful light.

Selected Bibliography

Works of Richard Eberhart

POETRY

A Bravery of Earth. New York: Jonathan Cape and Harrison Smith, 1930.
Reading the Spirit. New York: Oxford University Press, 1937.
Song and Idea. New York: Oxford University Press, 1942.
Poems, New and Selected. Norfolk, Conn.: New Directions, 1944.
Burr Oaks. New York: Oxford University Press, 1947.
Brotherhood of Man. Pawlet, Vt.: Banyan Press, 1949.
An Herb Basket. Cummington, Mass.: Cummington Press, 1950.
Selected Poems. New York: Oxford University Press, 1951.
Undercliff: Poems 1946–1953. New York: Oxford University Press, 1953.
Great Praises. New York: Oxford University Press, 1957.
Collected Poems 1930–1960. New York: Oxford University Press, 1960.
The Quarry: New Poems. New York: Oxford University Press, 1964.

PLAYS

Collected Verse Plays. Chapel Hill: University of North Carolina Press, 1962.

PROSE

"Empson's Poetry," in *Accent Anthology*, edited by Kerker Quinn and Charles Shattuck. New York: Harcourt, Brace, 1946. Pp. 571–88.
"Notes on Poetry," in *Mid-Century American Poets*, edited by John Ciardi. New York: Twayne, 1950. Pp. 225–29.
"The Stevens Prose," *Accent*, 12:122–25 (Spring 1952).
"Will and Psyche in Poetry," in *The Moment of Poetry*, edited by Don Cameron Allen. Baltimore: Johns Hopkins Press, 1962. Pp. 48–72.
"Tragedy as Limitation: Comedy as Control and Resolution," *Tulane Drama Review*, 6:3–14 (Summer 1962).
"Emerson and Wallace Stevens," *Literary Review*, 7:51–71 (Autumn 1963).
"On Theodore Roethke's Poetry," *Southern Review*, 1:612–20 (Summer 1965).
"How I Write Poetry," in *Poets on Poetry*, edited by Howard Nemerov. New York: Basic Books, 1966. Pp. 17–39.

RALPH J. MILLS, JR.

EDITED ANTHOLOGY OF POETRY

War and the Poet (with Selden Rodman). New York: Devin-Adair, 1945.

CURRENT AMERICAN REPRINT

Selected Poems 1930–1965. New York: New Directions. $1.75.

Critical Studies

Booth, Philip. "The Varieties of Poetic Experience," *Shenandoah,* 15:62–69 (Summer 1964).

Dickey, James. "Richard Eberhart," in *The Suspect in Poetry.* Madison, Minn.: The Sixties Press, 1964. Pp. 95–96.

Donoghue, Denis. *The Third Voice.* Princeton, N.J.: Princeton University Press, 1959. Pp. 194–95, 223–35.

———. "An Interview with Richard Eberhart," *Shenandoah,* 15:7–29 (Summer 1964).

Hall, Donald. "Method in Poetic Composition," *Paris Review,* 3:113–19 (Autumn 1953).

Hall, James. "Richard Eberhart: The Sociable Naturalist," *Western Review,* 18:315–21 (Summer 1954).

Hoffman, Daniel. "Hunting a Master Image: The Poetry of Richard Eberhart," *Hollins Critic,* 4:1–12 (October 1964).

Mills, Ralph J., Jr. "Richard Eberhart," in *Contemporary American Poetry.* New York: Random House, 1965. Pp. 9–31.

"On Richard Eberhart's 'Am I My Neighbor's Keeper?' " in *The Contemporary Poet as Artist and Critic,* edited by Anthony Ostroff. Boston: Little, Brown, 1964. Pp. 141–66. (This includes short essays by Louise Bogan, Philip Booth, and William Stafford, and Eberhart's reply.)

Rodman, Selden. "The Poetry of Richard Eberhart," *Perspectives U.S.A.,* 10:32–42 (Winter 1955).

Rosenthal, M. L. *The Modern Poets.* New York: Oxford University Press, 1960. Pp. 246–48.

Thorslev, Peter L., Jr. "The Poetry of Richard Eberhart," in *Poets in Progress,* edited by Edward B. Hungerford. Evanston, Ill.: Northwestern University Press, 1962. Pp. 73–91.